EYEWITNESS TO
THE ROLE OF WOMEN IN WORLD WAR I

BY JEANNE MARIE FORD

Published by The Child's World®
1980 Lookout Drive • Mankato, MN 56003-1705
800-599-READ • www.childsworld.com

Photographs ©: U.S. National Archives and Records Administration, cover, 1, 14; Museum of London/Heritage Images/Glow Images, 5; Charles Hilton DeWitt Girdwood/British Library, 6; Iconic Archive/Getty Images, 9; Everett Collection/ Newscom, 10; George Grantham Bain Collection/Library of Congress, 11; War Archive/Alamy, 12; Col. E. J. Parker/National Geographic Creative, 16; Library of Congress, 18; Bentley Archive/Popperfoto/Getty Images, 20; Everett Historical/ Shutterstock Images, 22, 23; Hulton Archive/Stringer/Getty Images, 24; Mirrorpix/ Newscom, 27; U.S. Naval History and Heritage Command Photograph, 28

ISBN 9781503816053

LCCN 2016945636

Printed in the United States of America
PA02317

ABOUT THE AUTHOR

Jeanne Marie Ford is an Emmy-winning TV scriptwriter and holds a master of fine arts degree in writing for children from Vermont College. She has written numerous children's books and articles. Ford also teaches college English. She lives in Maryland with her husband and two children.

TABLE OF
CONTENTS

FAST FACTS

What role did women play in World War I (1914-1918)?

- Women took over thousands of jobs men had held before the war.
- U.S. women served in the military for the first time.
- Many women worked as nurses or volunteered to help the wounded and hungry.
- Women also served as doctors and in the new field of physical therapy.

How was life at home affected by World War I?

- Food and money were often scarce.
- In Europe, cities were bombed and homes were destroyed.

Did any women fight in World War I?

- Some women fought on the European **front**.
- Women in the U.S. military worked to support the men who went into battle.

How did women's lives change as a result of World War I?

- Wartime work and military service created new job opportunities for women after the war.
- In places such as the United States and the United Kingdom, women's role in the war helped lead to expanded voting rights.

Chapter 1

A WORLD AT WAR

The winter sky was as gray as the soldiers' uniforms. Nellie Bly watched as soldiers first carried one coffin past her, then another. The long trenches where the men fought also looked like coffins, she thought.

Bly was famous for her daring undercover stunts as one of the first female newspaper reporters. Now, she stood on an Austrian battlefield on a cold December day in 1914. She faced her most dangerous assignment yet.

The enemy lay in wait on the other side of the hill. "I expect a **grenade** at any moment," a soldier warned her.[1] Despite the risk, Bly was determined to continue reporting on the horrors of World War I.

She noted that the once-green landscape was now littered with the bodies of dead soldiers. "The dead cannot be buried, the living cannot be aided until the rain of hellfire ceases," she wrote in an article for the *New York Evening Journal.* "I glance sadly at the dark, cold trenches. I say farewell to those I know. And the terrible booming and slaughter keep on."[2]

Bly knew that Americans across the Atlantic Ocean depended on her and her fellow reporters for news from the front lines. The United States was not yet involved in the war. But many Americans were recent **immigrants** from other countries. They still had family members living in Europe, where the battles were being fought. Some Americans supported the Allies, led by the British and French. Others supported the Central powers, led by Germany and Austria-Hungary.

While living in Vienna, Austria-Hungary, Bly saw the suffering of Austrian women whose husbands were killed in battle. She wrote articles urging readers to help them. When the United States joined the Allies on April 6, 1917, Austria-Hungary became the enemy. Because of Bly's support for the Austrian people, U.S. soldiers questioned her loyalty to the United States. She was not allowed to go home until they were satisfied that she supported the Allies' cause.

Bly spent much of her career fighting for women's rights. When she returned to the United States in 1919, she saw women's lives had changed greatly in the five years she had been gone.

Hundreds of thousands of men had gone to Europe to fight. Someone had to fill the empty jobs. Allied women became nurses, doctors, and ambulance drivers.

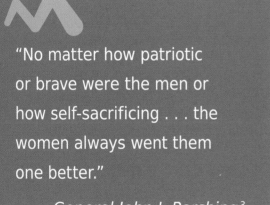

"No matter how patriotic or brave were the men or how self-sacrificing . . . the women always went them one better."

—*General John J. Pershing*[3]

Nellie Bly's real name was Elizabeth Cochran Seaman. It was ▶ thought to be improper at the time for a woman to write using her real name.

▲ **Operators for the U.S. Army Signal Corps helped improve communication on the Western front. Operators spoke English and French.**

Women also became airplane builders, factory workers, fishers, and farmers.

During World War I, women were also allowed to serve in the U.S. military for the first time. Elizabeth Shoemaker wanted desperately to become a U.S. Marine but failed the entry test. She was so disappointed that she decided to try again. She went back the next day wearing new clothes and with her hair in a different style. The **colonel** recognized her. She thought he would not let her take the test. But he admired her determination. He let her take the test again. This time she passed.

The war changed many people's ideas of what a woman's role should be. Women's wartime service paved the way for new rights and responsibilities that have endured.

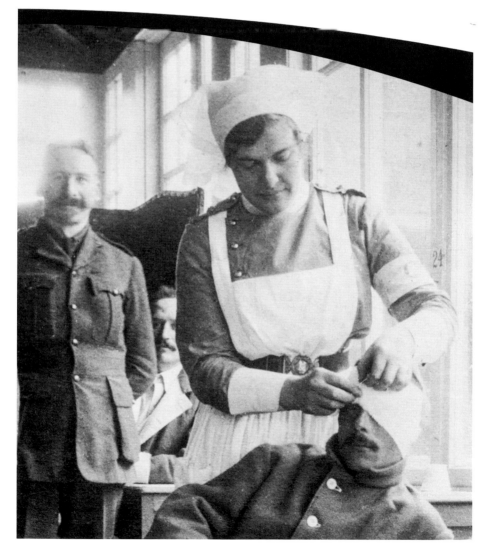

▲ **World War I was the first time U.S. Army and U.S. Navy nurses served overseas.**

Chapter 2

WAR AT HOME

Every morning at 5:00, Gertrude Cursley left her home in central England to board a train to the Chilwell factory. When she arrived, she changed from her long skirt to a work suit and rubber boots. With time, her skin had begun to turn yellow. The color came from the chemicals she worked with every day. It did not come off, even after a bath.

Cursley had four young children at home, and her husband, Harry, was fighting in the war. She was usually tired even before she began her long shift. Her job was to fill heavy bombshells with explosive powder. The powder was made of sulfur, which smelled like rotten eggs. Workers had to shout to be heard over the noisy machinery. But Cursley was proud of her work making bombs the soldiers needed to fight the war.

On July 1, 1918, the Chilwell factory exploded. Everyone inside was killed. Cursley's family got a letter notifying them of her death. The phrase *his death* was crossed out in pen, and the word *his* was replaced with *her*.

Like Cursley, Kitty Eckersley worked in a British factory while her husband fought in the war. She was pregnant with their first child. Her due date was two months away when she received a letter from her husband's sergeant. She could not bring herself to read the sad news she knew it contained. Eckersley ran outside in her nightgown, barefooted, to her neighbor's house. Her neighbor had to tell her that her husband had died. "The world had come to an end for me," Eckersley said, "'cos I'd lost all that I'd loved."[4]

Eckersley was one of thousands of war **widows** who raised their children alone. With their husbands gone, many mothers did not have enough money to care for their families. Shoppers stood in long lines to buy supplies from shelves that were nearly bare. Items such as bread, sugar, and meat were **rationed**. In Germany, some families had only potatoes to eat. When these ran out, desperate women attacked soldiers to get food for their children.

"Who works, fights."

—*David Lloyd George,*
British Prime Minister[5]

Bombs rained down on large European cities and killed people in their own homes. Women and children learned to use gas masks to protect themselves from chemical weapons. It was a time of terrible suffering, especially for those who lived in Europe. For some women in the workforce, it was also a time of opportunities that would not have come in peacetime. Nearly every life was touched by the war in some way.

◀ **Women took on physically demanding jobs during World War I that before the war were thought to be too strenuous for them.**

15

Chapter 3

HELPERS

Helen Purviance could hear machine-gun fire as she knelt in the dirt beside a small stove. She was a Salvation Army volunteer from Indiana. She had just finished collecting eggs from the nearby French village. She wanted to make a surprise treat for the Allied soldiers.

Purviance did not have a rolling pin. So she patted the dough into small, circular pieces.

She then fried them in a skillet. Dozens of batches later, she had made 150 doughnuts. The soldiers were thrilled by her surprise. They were so eager to eat the doughnuts that they used twigs to pull them from the hot pan.

Soon the unit was ordered to move closer to the battlefield. Purviance and three other female workers went, too. The commander gave them gas masks, helmets, and guns for protection. They slept in **dugouts** and cooked for the soldiers as enemy airplanes flew overhead.

Next, Purviance volunteered to help in a hospital. She bathed wounded men. She made them soup and hot chocolate. She wrote letters home for soldiers who could no longer hold pens.

One day she went outside to get some fresh air. But she felt guilty taking a walk for pleasure. So she gathered bright flowers and laid them on the graves of U.S. soldiers nearby. She carried the rest of the pink and red flowers back to the wounded soldiers to cheer them up. Twice during her tour, Purviance was nearly killed by bombs. But she continued serving. By the end of the war, she had handed out more than 1 million doughnuts to the troops.

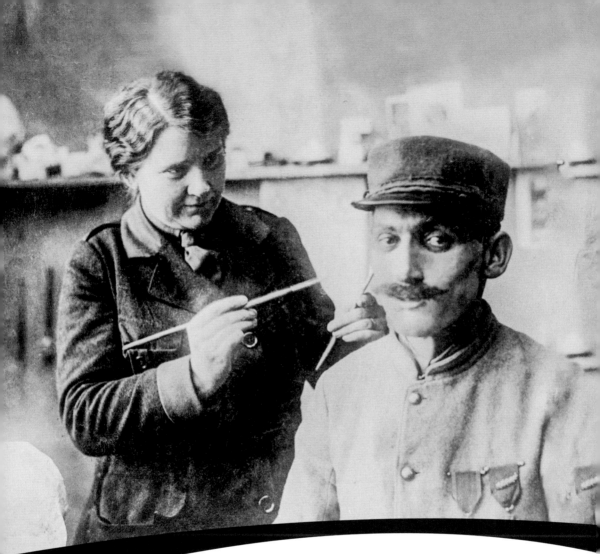

▲ **In a year and a half, Ladd helped sculpt more than 100 masks for wounded soldiers.**

Purviance was one of thousands of U.S. volunteers who traveled to the war front. Many went before the United States entered the war. They worked for organizations such as the YMCA, the Salvation Army, and the Red Cross.

They lived in small huts and endured bitter cold. Some even had to pay for their own travel and buy their own supplies.

Anna Coleman Ladd was a U.S. sculptor and Red Cross volunteer in Paris, France. Soldiers with terrible facial wounds came to her when doctors could not help them. She set up a cheerful studio to make the injured men comfortable. There, Ladd made plaster images of their faces. She used these to carefully sculpt copper masks. She painted them to match each soldier's skin color. Then, she crafted details such as eyelashes from real hair. Of course, these masks could not replace the soldiers' own faces. But her creations let the men go out in the world and live more normal lives. One wounded soldier told her, "Thanks to you, I can live again."[6]

"For the first time in my life I feel that I am a necessity in this world. There is no feeling more glorious!"

—Crystal Waters, YMCA entertainer who sang for the troops[7]

Chapter 4

HEALERS

D r. Elsie Inglis was walking outside a Serbian hospital in the fall of 1915 when a bomb exploded in the sky above her. When her ears stopped ringing, she turned to the nurse beside her and said, "We're having some experiences, aren't we?"[8]

Inglis had been saving lives for more than 20 years when World War I began. She was one of the first female doctors in Scotland.

She had started a medical college and hospital for women. A skilled surgeon, she volunteered to treat wounded soldiers in the war. "My good lady, go home and sit still," a member of the Scottish War Office told her.[9]

She did not go home. And she did not sit still. After running a hospital for Allied troops in Serbia, she served in Russia as a field surgeon. "We were not called to the colors," said fellow doctor Esther Pohl Lovejoy, "but we decided to serve anyway."[10]

Although female doctors such as Inglis and Lovejoy were rare, nearly all nurses were women. Their work was difficult. They saw a great deal of blood and filth, suffering and death. Sometimes the nurses went weeks without rest. They wore long underwear and knitted caps to guard against the cold weather.

"When a nurse takes the pulse of a wounded sleeping man and he wakes just enough to say 'Mother,' she goes to pieces in her heart."

—U.S. Army nurse Julia C. Stimson[11]

Nurses twisted dirty hair on top of their heads. They went without warm water to bathe in, just as the soldiers did. With too much work and too little sleep, many doctors and nurses became sick themselves. Inglis was one of them. She hid her illness and did not stop working until the day before she died.

▲ **Nurses often worked in trains and ships that transported the wounded to hospitals.**

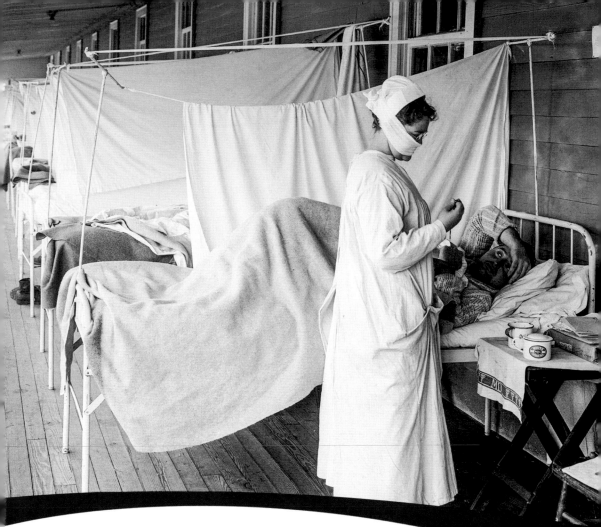

▲ **In addition to caring for those hurt in battle, nurses also treated patients affected by a deadly flu epidemic.**

Nurse Nellie Dingley fell ill during the deadly influenza **epidemic** of 1918. Shortly before she died, she wrote to a friend: "Regardless of anything else that has been or should come into my life, my work here in France will ever remain the pot of gold at the end of the rainbow for me."[12]

Chapter 5

SOLDIERS AND SAILORS

Bernice Duncan Smith was riding a streetcar to work in Los Angeles, California, when she saw the newspaper headline. The navy was letting women join! Women had never been admitted to the U.S. military before. Eager to serve her country, she rushed to sign up.

"We don't take women," a clerk at the office quickly told her. She held up the paper.

"This newspaper says they are **enlisting** women in Washington, DC, and if they can do it, so can you," she argued. He was not persuaded, so she continued. "Sir, if I were a man, I would join the navy. This is the first time in history that my family hasn't been represented in an American war, and you've just got to take me."[13] Days later, they did.

Smith was able to serve thanks to Secretary of the Navy Josephus Daniels. Daniels knew he needed more sailors to fight the war. He noted there was no rule saying women could not join. He decided women could and should join the navy. More than 10,000 women would enlist before the end of World War I.

These women entered a navy run by men. When they arrived for their medical checkups, they were told to strip off their clothes. They shivered in their towels as they were herded into one room, where they waited to be examined by male doctors. At first, the navy had no uniforms for them to wear. It was even difficult to decide what to call them. Men were **yeomen**, so Daniels decided the women should be yeomen (F). The *F* stood for *female*.

In Europe, Maria Bochkareva joined the Russian army to serve beside her husband. When he was killed, she kept fighting.

She persuaded 2,000 other women to fight with her. Reporter Bessie Beatty watched the female soldiers in action. She wrote, "Women have the courage, the endurance, and even the strength for fighting. The Russians have demonstrated that, and, if necessary, all the other women in the world can demonstrate it."[14]

> "It was such an honor to be one of the first women in the navy. It was a beautiful part of my life."
>
> —Mary Margaret Fitzgerald, Yeoman (F)[15]

But unlike the Russians, women in the U.S. Navy did not go into battle. They worked many jobs that women typically held, such as typists and telephone operators. They were also codebreakers, fingerprint clerks, mechanics, and truck drivers.

Many people did not like the idea of women in the military. The brother of at least one yeoman (F) got into a fistfight with a man who insulted them. But as the women did their jobs, the public grew more comfortable with the idea of female soldiers and sailors. The marines began to **recruit** women in 1918, shortly before the war ended.

And then the war was over. Army nurse Laura Frost was serving in Belgium when the gunfire stopped. She described the sudden silence on that November morning as peace fell over the land. The Allies had won the war.

▲ **As the losses in the war mounted, Russian women formed their own military battalions.**

▲ **Yeomen (F) march in a naval parade in New York City in May 1919.**

When Frost arrived in New York harbor, she flung her hat with joy toward the Statue of Liberty. Bands played, and crowds gathered to greet the ship full of victorious soldiers.

"You more than came up to my expectations," Daniels told the women who had served in the navy. "I feel it is one of the greatest honors in my life to have been associated with you in the days of emergency in war."

Nonetheless, Smith and the rest of the yeomen (F) were released from the military within a year of the war's end.[16]

Smith and her fellow yeomen (F) readjusted to life outside the military. But they had played an important part in changing people's minds about women's roles in society. In 1919 all U.S. women were granted the right to vote. And although many left their wartime jobs, some continued to work for the government. Others pursued college degrees or careers. And when World War II (1939–1945) broke out 20 years later, the idea of women in the military was much more easily accepted.

Smith tried to rejoin the U.S. Navy during World War II. They told her she was too old. She joined the army instead. She proudly served beside her son.

THINK ABOUT IT

- Why do you think many people resisted having women in the military?
- Why were women eager to help with the war effort?
- How did society change when women were given more opportunities to work outside the home?

GLOSSARY

colonel (KUR-nuhl): A colonel is a high-ranking military officer. In the U.S. Army, only a general outranks a colonel.

dugouts (DUHG-outs): Dugouts are underground shelters. Many soldiers slept in dugouts during the war.

enlisting (en-LIST-ing): Enlisting means joining the military. Many women began enlisting during World War I.

epidemic (ep-i-DEM-ik): An epidemic is an illness that spreads quickly to many people. The flu epidemic of 1918 was very deadly.

front (FRUHNT): The front is the area where two military forces face off in combat. Medical workers were often located near the front to quickly help injured soldiers.

grenade (gruh-NADE): A grenade is a small bomb that is thrown. Grenade explosions caused many injuries in the war.

immigrants (IM-i-grunts): Immigrants are people who move to another country to live. Many immigrants to the United States in the early 1900s came from Germany.

rationed (RASH-und): When something is rationed, people may have only limited amounts. Food was rationed in World War I so soldiers would have enough to eat.

recruit (ri-KROOT): To recruit is to ask someone to join a group. Many women helped recruit others into the navy.

widows (WID-ohs): Widows are women whose husbands have died. Many women became widows as a result of World War I.

yeomen (YO-men): Yeomen are navy clerks. Female yeomen were not allowed to go to sea during World War I.

SOURCE NOTES

1. Nelly Bly. "Perils of the Cholera." *Nellie Bly Online*. Tri Fritz, n.d. Web. 18 May 2016.

2. Nelly Bly. "Dead Strew Trenches." *Nellie Bly Online*. Tri Fritz, n.d. Web. 18 May 2016.

3. Elizabeth Foxwell. *In Their Own Words: American Women in World War I*. Waverly, TN: Oconee Spirit, 2015. Kindle file.

4. Kate Adie. "What I'll Be Remembering This Armistice Day." *Telegraph*. Telegraph Media Group, 1 Nov. 2016. Web. 18 May 2016.

5. Lettie Gavin. *American Women in World War I: They Also Served*. Niwot, CO: UP of Colorado, 1997. Print. X.

6. Michael E. Ruane. "An American Sculptor's Masks Restored French Soldiers Disfigured in World War I." *Washington Post*. Washington Post, 22 Sep. 2014. Web. 18 May 2016.

7. Elizabeth Foxwell. *In Their Own Words: American Women in World War I*. Waverly, TN: Oconee Spirit, 2015. Kindle file.

8. Lucy Inglis. "Elsie Inglis, the Suffragette Physician." *Lancet*. Elsevier, 8 Nov. 2014. Web. 18 May 2016.

9. Ibid.

10. Lettie Gavin. *American Women in World War I: They Also Served*. Niwot, CO: UP of Colorado, 1997. Print. IX.

11. Julia Catherine Stimson. "Letter from Julia Catherine Stimson to Her Parents, 1917." *Women in America*. Primary Source Media, 1999. Web. 18 Jul. 2016.

12. Lettie Gavin. *American Women in World War I: They Also Served*. Niwot, CO: UP of Colorado, 1997. Print. 63.

13. Ibid. 14.

14. Bessie Beatty. "The Red Heart of Russia." *Archive.org*. Internet Archive, 29 Jun. 2007. Web. 18 May 2016.

15. Lettie Gavin. *American Women in World War I: They Also Served*. Niwot, CO: UP of Colorado, 1997. Print. 12.

16. Ibid. 15.

TO LEARN MORE

Books

Adams, Simon. *World War I*. New York: DK, 2014.

Bearce, Stephanie. *Spies, Secret Missions, & Hidden Facts from World War I*. Waco, TX: Prufrock, 2015.

Hagar, Erin. *Doing Her Bit*. Watertown, MA: Charlesbridge, 2016.

Web Sites

Visit our Web site for links about women in World War I:

childsworld.com/links

Note to Parents, Teachers, and Librarians: We routinely verify our Web links to make sure they are safe and active sites. So encourage your readers to check them out!

INDEX